All rights reserved under International and Pan-American Copy-
right Conventions. Published in the United States by Pantheon
Books, a division of Random House, Inc., New York, and simultane-
ously in Canada by Random House of Canada Limited, Toronto.
Originally published in Japanese as *Goka o Mita* and in English translation as *Unforgettable Fire* by Nippon Hoso Shuppan Kyokai, Tokyo.

English translation by World Friendship Center in Hiroshima,
supervised by Howard Schonberger and Leona Row.

LIBRARY OF CONGRESS CATALOGING IN PUBLICATION DATA
Main entry under title:
Unforgettable fire.
    Translation of Gōka o mita.
    Includes index.
    1. Hiroshima—Bombardment, 1945—Pictorial works.
I. Nippon Hōsō Kyōkai.
D767.25.H6G13   1981   940.54'26   80-8647
ISBN 0-394-51585-4
ISBN 0-394-74823-9 (pbk.)

Manufactured in the United States of America
FIRST AMERICAN EDITION

CONTENTS

PREFACE   5

HIROSHIMA ON THAT DAY   6

One   THE BOMB AND I   11

Two   BOMB FLASH! 8:15 A.M.   14

Three WHAT I SAW ON THAT DAY   20

Four   THE ENFLAMED CITY   29

Five   WHERE IS MY CHILD? WHERE IS MY WIFE?   51

Six   HANDS OF HELP   76

Seven THE CITY OF THE DEAD   96

       THE PICTURES ABOUT THE ATOMIC BOMB   105

       INDEX   111

The collection of pictures about the A-Bomb experience as drawn by the survivors was started by Nippon Hoso Kyokai (NHK), Japan Broadcasting Corporation. The impetus for this project came when one survivor brought a hand-drawn picture to NHK's Hiroshima office. The collection was introduced on television and exhibited at the Peace Culture Center in Hiroshima City August 1 to August 6, 1975. The exhibition hall was filled with excitement and deep emotion. A notebook in which visitors could write their impressions had been placed in the hall and was quickly filled. More impression notes continued to come in until more than ten notebooks were piled up. Some of these notes urged that the pictures be displayed not only in Japan but also in foreign countries in order that this cruel situation should be widely known.

Thirty years have passed since the A-Bomb was dropped. The memory of how things were in Hiroshima at that time is being forgotten. It is therefore necessary to appeal to the people of Japan and of the world that there be no "No More Hiroshima." The pictures in this book are only a small part of those which were sent in by the survivors. To publish a collection of these pictures as a book is very significant, since we are living in a world in which the diffusion of nuclear weapons is threatening the existence of all humanity.

The pictures are a vivid documentary of the miserable scenes of that day, although thirty years have passed. The memories, etched in the minds of the survivors, are unforgettable! Photographs cannot express the strong impressions which these pictures, drawn by the actual survivors, portray. We hope that all of you can understand the heart-felt cries of the survivors as you look at the individual pictures of this collection. We thank those of you who participated in the movement "Let Us Leave for Posterity Pictures about the Atomic-Bomb Drawn by Citizens" and helped in so many different ways.

NHK Chugoku Area Chief
SOJI MATSUMOTO

June, 1975

HIROSHIMA ON THAT DAY

That morning......

On August 6, 1945, the morning started with a cloudless blue sky characteristic of the Inland Sea's summer. In March the big Tokyo air raid had killed 120,000 citizens. Many other cities in Japan were also violently bombed and burned by the American air attacks so that many non-combatants continued to be cruelly killed. In April American armed forces landed on Okinawa and the whole island became a battlefield. 90,000 Japanese soldiers were killed and 100,000 civilians died. Japanese people cried loudly that they would fight a decisive battle on the mainland.

Hiroshima remained unharmed. A wild rumor spread that the Americans were not bombing in Hiroshima because it was a religious city with many Buddhist believers. Though not known at the time, in fact, the American military had ordered that Hiroshima be spared from bombing raids in order to later calculate accurately the full effects of the A-Bomb.

Hiroshima developed on the delta at the mouth of the Ota River that ran from the Chugoku mountains into the Seto Inland Sea. In line with the Meiji government's policy to make the country rich and the army strong, Hiroshima became a strategic center for the Japanese military. From Hiroshima's Ujina Port soldiers recruited from all over Japan were sent to battle on the Asian continent. As World War II continued, Hiroshima developed into a major military city.

Before daybreak of August 6 an air raid alarm was given in Hiroshima. At 7 : 00 A.M. another air raid alarm was sounded. But at 7 : 31 A.M. the all clear was given. Soldiers at the anti-aircraft machine guns on the roofs of the military installations and munitions factories were released by an air defense order.

Just before the fateful moment the seven rivers which ran through the city looked stagnant because of the high tide and reflected the deep-blue of the summer sky. Wearing work clothes and gaiters, with air defense hoods thrown back, people were running on the big and small bridges throughout the city. One of these was the Aioi Bridge, an unusual T-type bridge. It was the target of the A-Bomb. The mobilized students, even school girls, were hurrying to the munitions factories by streetcar. A horse-drawn farmer's cart, taking nightsoil from the city to outlying farms,

passed by at a leisurely pace with a clop-clop noise. Small clouds of dust rose here and there among the crowded, tile-roofed houses. These showed that work had begun on pulling down evacuated buildings to make compulsory firelanes. Members of the Women's Society of Labor Service, National Volunteers from the suburban districts, and junior high school students put their lunches in the shade of nearby trees before beginning a long day of sweaty, dusty work.

In public offices and businesses workers had begun their jobs after their section chiefs had given their morning instructions. In public schools morning assemblies had begun because even during summer vacation, students who had not been evacuated had lessons there. Little children were busy playing in the streets. There were even foreigners in Hiroshima. Several thousand Koreans who had been taken from their country were working as forced laborers in an armament factory. There were some foreign students from Southeast Asian countries. And there were even Americans, POW Army pilots who had been shot down. Suddenly a bell rang in the broadcasting department of NHK. It was a warning given from the Army Headquarters of Chugoku District. The radio announcer began to read the bulletin, "Chugoku District Army Information. Three enemy airplanes have been spotted over the Saijo area..." Just then there was a dreadful shaking and loud crash of iron and concrete. The announcer was thrown into the air.

The Flash : 8 : 15

The A-Bomb, which was nicknamed "Little Boy", was dropped from the B–29, Enola Gay. It exploded 570 meters above the ground with a light blue flash. The diameter of the fireball was 100 meters and the temperature at its center was 300,000° C. Soon after the explosion black and white smoke covered the whole city and rose thousands of meters high. The pressure of the blast directly under the center of the explosion was from 4.5 to 6.7 tons per square meter. Wooden houses within a radius of two kilometers of the hypocenter collapsed and completely burned from the wind and heat. The fires continued for two days. Some people who were near the center of the explosion literally evaporated and only their shadows remained ; others were turned to charred

corpses. Those who survived were badly burned. Usually their clothes were scorched and burned so they were practically naked. Their skin peeled off and hung down. They rushed to nearby fire prevention water boxes and river banks seeking water. Friends and relatives trapped under collapsed houses were crying for help. But flames surrounded them so closely that they were about to burn.

Later large black drops of rain poured down. It was a deadly rain which contained mud, ash, and other radioactive fallout. Through burning flames and pouring black rain there was an endless line of injured people heading for the outskirts of the city. The burns on their hands made the skin hang down. Their hands looked like those of ghosts.

"Give me water."

The security functions of the army, police, prefecture, and city agencies practically ceased. Under such circumstances medical treatment was started by doctors and nurses who were injured themselves. Damage to nearby army posts was rather slight and so soldiers from them first began the relief job. Hospitals soon became full, so public schools around the city were used as first-aid stations. They were also crowded by the rush of wounded persons. Countless dead bodies and seriously wounded people, who barely breathed, were left on the road or the river-banks of the city. Medical supplies were used up immediately because of the unimaginable number of wounded persons. The untreated people took their last breath moaning, "Give me water." What is now called radiation sickness soon appeared. People began suffering from diarrhea as if they had dysentery, losing clumps of their hair, and developing purple colored spots on their skin which made them look like a map. Such people soon died, their bodies full of big maggots they were too weak to remove.

Those who were looking for their relatives walked around in the still smoldering city with the rescue parties. What they saw were dead bodies piled up on the ground and filling up the rivers. Figures of mothers who died protecting their own children were especially heartbreaking. People were deeply scarred by the indiscriminate cruelty of the new styled bomb and the dreadfulness of war itself.

Among those who entered the city later, there were a large number of people who were affected by lingering radioactivity, and died. Cremation of dead bodies continued for many days throughout the city. On top of some wood dead bodies were piled up, oil poured on them, and a fire was lit. The smell of dead bodies and the wail of sutra-chanting spread over the vast scorched desolation.

And on August 9, the second A-Bomb was dropped on Nagasaki.

Appeal for Peace

Although many believed Hiroshima would be barren for seventy years, amidst the ruins canna lilies bloomed and grass flourished from the effects of radioactivity. On the first anniversary of the A-Bomb a "Peace Revival Festival" was organized by citizen groups in the city where only shacks stood. Although under the American occupation speeches and gatherings were strictly controlled, the festival was attended by thousands holding flags draped in black and placards saying "World Peace from Hiroshima". The following year, August 6, 1947, Mayor of Hiroshima, Mr. Hamai, read the first "Peace Declaration" at the renamed "Peace Festival". He declared: "Those who have experienced and fully realized the anguish and sin of war would denounce war absolutely as the ultimate agony, and wish for peace most passionately."

Despite such pleas for peace, the Soviet Union proclaimed its possession of the A-Bomb in September 1949; in January 1950, the President of the United States announced that he had ordered the start of H-Bomb production. Five months later, the Korean War broke out. England also began atomic development. On March 1, 1954, a tuna fishing boat from Yaizu, Shizuoka Prefecture, *Fifth Lucky Dragon*, while operating near Bikini Atoll in the South Pacific, was showered with radioactive fallout from an H-Bomb test conducted by the United States. The chief radio operator of the boat, Mr. Aikichi Kuboyama, died in the fall of that year from the radiation effects of this weapon, one 600 times more powerful than the A-Bomb dropped on Hiroshima.

The Yaizu City Council passed a resolution at the end of March, 1954, against nuclear weapons and this appeal met with an immediate response from many other local governments in Japan. Both Houses of the Diet passed resolutions in April to ban the use of atomic weapons. At the same time, a movement to circulate a petition calling for a ban on nuclear weapons arose among the women of Hiroshima and of Suginami Ward of Tokyo. This non-partisan movement became part of a strong current which spread all over the nation. Twenty million signatures were collected and Gensuikyo, the Japan Council Against A- and H-Bombs, was established.

When Gensuikyo divided into factions resulting from conflicts over the U. S.–Japan Security Treaty and the resumption of nuclear testing by the Soviet Union, many citizens of Hiroshima were discouraged and silent. But in August, 1966, their hopes were rekindled by an NHK-Hiroshima television program which attempted to answer many simple questions about the A-Bomb explosion. How many people were in the hypocenter area at the time of the explosion? Where were they from? What kind of work did they do? What kind of buildings were there? Growing out of this program, television journalists, scientists at the Research Institute for Nuclear Medicine and Biology of Hiroshima University, and a large number of ordinary citizens, joined in a movement to recover information about and to reproduce on a scale model the hypocenter area. The movement would also make an appeal for peace based on the survivors' experiences of the first A-Bomb explosion in history. The City of Hiroshima took over this movement and prepared a report to the United Nations as part of the activities of the 30th anniversary year. Even after careful investigation, the estimate of 240,000 casualties from the A-Bomb is not considered reliable.

Last year the movement of "Pictures about the A-Bomb Drawn by Hiroshima Citizens" was triggered by a single drawing brought to NHK-Hiroshima and the enthusiasm of Hiroshima's people. This is a new civic movement not seen since the movement to replicate the hypocenter area. (Sources: "A-Bomb Record of Hiroshima" by Hiroshima City; "History of Hiroshima Prefecture-A-Bomb Materials Volume" by Hiroshima Prefecture; "The A-Bomb Hypocenter" by Dr. Kiyoshi Shimizu; a large number of drawings contributed by the citizens.)

One   **THE BOMB AND I**

Goro Kiyoyoshi age 80 (283)

This is a picture from Mt. Futaba which overlooks Hiroshima city. Standing on the hill I could see the shrine at its foot engulfed in flames and Shukkeien Garden burning between two branches of the Ota River. The fire extended to the Hiroshima Castle. Above the city was a mushroom cloud from the Atomic Bomb.

11

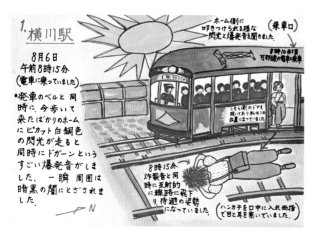

At Yokogawa Station August 6, 1945, 8 : 15 A.M.

I got on a streetcar of the Kabe line about 8 : 10 A.M. The door was open and I was standing there. As I heard the starting bell ring, I saw a silver flash and heard an explosion over the platform on which I had just walked. Next moment everything went dark.

Instinctively I jumped down to the track and braced myself against it. Putting a handkerchief into my mouth, I covered my eyes and ears with my hands.

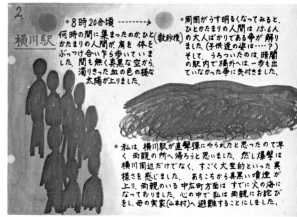

About 8 : 20 A.M. at Yokogawa Station

I do not know when they had gathered, but a crowd of people were reeling and colliding with each other. Soon the sun appeared blood-red in the dark sky. When it became a little lighter around me I saw a group of 15 or 16 adults. "Where had the children gone?" I wondered. Black smoke was rising here and there and Nakahiro-cho where my parents lived was already in flame. Apologizing in my heart to my parents I decided to seek shelter.

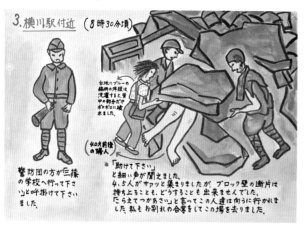

Around Yokogawa Station about 8 : 30 A.M.

I had worn a white blouse with a blue striped pattern that day. The back fell apart later when I washed it.

A civilian guard told us, "Please go to the school in Misasa."

I heard a woman saying in a small voice, "Please help me." Four or five people got together immediately to help her. But we couldn't move the concrete block off her no matter how we tried. Saying, "Forgive us", the others left her as she was and went away. I prayed for her and then also left.

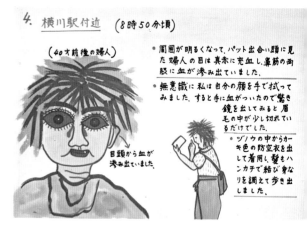

Near Yokogawa Station about 8 : 50 A.M.

A lady about 40 years old was bleeding from her eyes.

It was getting light and I met a lady whose eyes were bloodshot. The blood was oozing down from the corners of the eyes along both sides of her nose.

Unconsciously I wiped my face with my hands and I was surprised to see that there was blood on them. I got my mirror out of my pocket and looked into it. I found only a small cut on my eyebrow.

I took my khaki air-raid dress out of my bag and put it on, tied my hair with a handkerchief, dressed myself neatly and started walking.

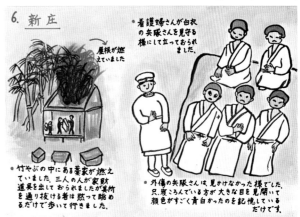

The river bank from Misasa to Mitaki

A girl was standing in the middle of the road staring vacantly. Strange to say, her clothes were not tattered. She was eight years old. The wound on her head looked like a cracked pomegranate. Silently I carried her on my back and headed in the direction of the Ota River.

Then I heard a girl's voice clearly from behind a tree. "Help me, please." Her back was completely burned and the skin peeled off and was hanging down from her hips.

Shinjo near Gion Bridge

A straw-thatched cottage among bamboo bushes was burning. Three persons were taking furniture out. The passers-by did not help them. They glanced at them and silently continued on their way. A nurse was standing near the soldiers in white as if she was watching over them. The soldiers did not appear wounded to me. What I remember is just the pale face and the wide-opened eyes of one soldier lying there.

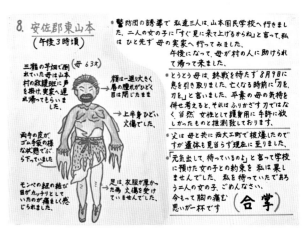

At the bank of the Nagatsuka around 9:40 A.M.

The refugees walked in procession along the bank of the river toward Gion. There was nobody who was wearing good clothes or was without wounds except me. Everyone was in rags and hurt. I walked feeling guilty because only I still had nice clothes and was not wounded.

A woman was walking, crying, "Can anyone help me?" The flesh of her side was scooped out and bleeding profusely and I could see her ribs. A man began to walk beside her, saying, "Everyone has the same pain as you have. Endure it and we will seek a shelter".

Higashi Yamamoto, Asa County
My mother, 63 years old

While lying on a potato farm in Mitaki my mother had asked the rescue party from her village for help and they brought her home.

Her face was larger than usual, her lips were badly swollen, and her eyes remained closed. The skin of both her hands was hanging loose as if it were rubber gloves. The upper part of her body was badly burned.

My mother passed away on August 9 before seeing the war end. My father who was in Daiku-cho at the time of the explosion, just as my mother was, disappeared and we have never even found his body.

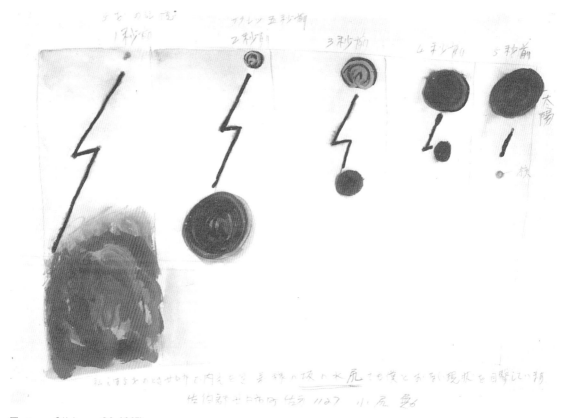

Tsutomu Ojiri age 36 (867)

(Top row of circles represents the sun compared to growing size of fireball in bottom row.)

I saw the explosion in Hatsukaichi about 10 miles away when I was five years old. This is the way I remembered the explosion in the five seconds before the sound reached me. (from right to left) One second before, two seconds, three seconds, four seconds, five seconds. I imagine others saw the same scene from Mizujiri near the Inland Sea at Saka-machi.

悲しいあの日の一瞬　原爆が裂烈した
幾人かの人々が見た　　瞬間の記憶図
ことであらうと思う

広島県佐伯郡大野町　五

當時＝広島県佐伯郡大野村　中山　　⊕　の地点より見る　　⌗＝大竹海軍強開兵舎

Kiyoshi Inoue age 51 (532)

How many people saw the explosion at that terrible instant ! I saw the explosion about 20 kilometers away at the red circle on the picture. The other spot on the picture marks the barracks for the Navy at the Otake evacuation center.

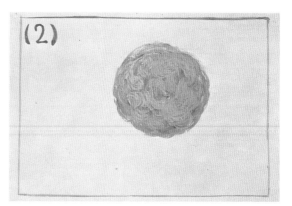

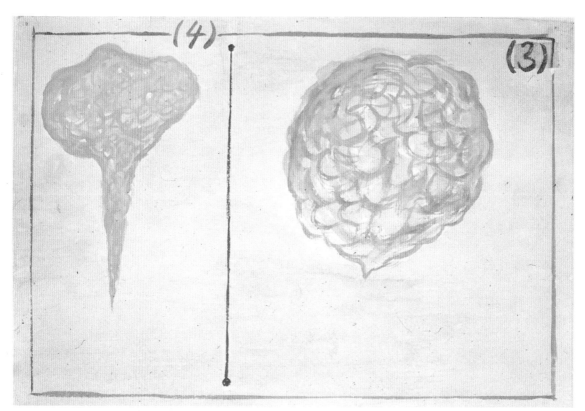

Kiyoshi Inoue age 51 (533–535)

Sumako Yamada age 54 (439–441)

八月六日午前八時十五分瞬間ピカ！
プシーッと言ふ音と共にあたり一面ピンクと
水色の光線でおおわれた。
此の後黒い雨が降る

甲斐中町にて

Yoshiaki Tamaru age 66 (411)

Koi Nakamachi

At 8 : 15 A.M. on August 6 everything
was instantly covered with pink and light blue
rays. There was a strange whooshing sound
and then black rain came down.

August 6 around 8 : 20 A.M.

I had a view of Hijiyama from Hijiyama
Elementary School. Going out of an air-raid
shelter I could see the mushroom cloud beyond
the mountain. The top was narrower than
below but it was getting bigger as I watched.
I wondered what the red smoke was.

18

Hidehiko Okazaki age 50 (646)

8月6日 8時20分頃 比治山小学校より比治山を望む

防空壕をおると比治山の向うにきのこ雲があった。先は高いためか下より小さく見えたが見る〱大きくなってしまった。ところどころの紅色の煙は何だったろう？

Takehiko Sakai age 53 (294–295)

The disaster in the old Fukuya Department Store which I saw from the fourth floor of new Fukuya store in Hacchobori about twenty or thirty minutes after the A-Bomb had dropped.
▶

Tomoe Harada age 52 (475)

Setsuko Yamamoto age 46 (414)

(415)

A desperate escape from the streetcar at Hakushima line just after the A-Bomb explosion.

(caption at bottom of page for lower middle picture)

What I still cannot forget is that my scissors and my lunch box were both thrown onto the floor from my emergency bag when I fell down on the floor. Although they were within my reach, I escaped leaving them behind. I have always regretted not bringing them. Why didn't I stretch out my hands to take them ? I did not have enough presence of mind and I am still heartsick. That pair of scissors sent by my friend in Hawaii was a good remembrance to me. It was sharp, shiny, and never rusted. I have many good memories of my lunch box, too.

(on picture, left side)

I smlled and tasted the black rain on my hand. Parents were looking for their children and children were crying for their parents. Houses along the street were burning. I went down to the river from the back-gate and washed my hands and feet, and dampened my clothes for the next air-raid. In the excitement I urinated in my clothes and then washed them. There were countless people on the riverbank.

24

Name withheld by request (250)

(top middle picture)

August 6 a few minutes after 8 : 00 A.M.
(Black ink is used to draw the scene before the A-Bomb ; red ink immediately after the A-Bomb exploded.)

The vice-principal who came into the classroom immediately after the A-Bomb had lost his glasses, his clothes were torn off, and his arms, bloody and skinned, hung down by his side. His face was burned black. I met him at the doorway.

I sighed with relief and sat down at a desk when the air-raid alarm, which was given during the night, was called off. Suddenly there was an unusual blue light. It was hot and painful. Numerous pieces of glass scattered and attacked me on my head, face, and back. When I stood up and took a few steps toward the entrance, I was pushed from behind by a strong force and fell down by the doorway.

Torako Hironaka age 63 (183)

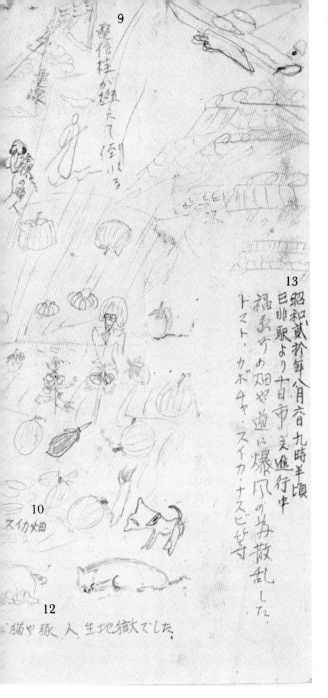

1. Some burned work-clothes.
2. People crying for help with their heads, shoulders, or the soles of their feet injured by fragments of broken window glass. Glass fragments were scattered everywhere.
3. She was crying, saying "Aigo! Aigo!" (a Korean expression of sorrow)
4. A burning pine tree.
5. A naked woman.
6. Naked girls crying "Stupid America!"
7. I was crouching in a puddle for fear of being shot by a machine gun. My breasts were torn.
8. Burned down electric power lines.
9. A telephone pole had burned and fallen down.
10. A field of watermelons.
11. A dead horse.
12. What with dead cats, pigs, and people, it was just a hell on earth.
13. 9 : 30 A.M. August 6, 1945 I was on the way from Koi station to Tokaichi. These are tomatoes, pumpkins, watermelons, eggplants, etc. which were scattered on the field or roads in Fukushima-cho because of the blast.

Near Takanobashi a fire had already broken out around 8 : 25 A.M. A woman's cry for help saddened me as I could not help her.

Kanichi Ito age 72 (350)

Please help this child !
Someone, please help this child.
Please help !
Someone, please.

Hatsuji Takeuchi age 60 (896)

Yoshiko Michitsuji age 51 (407)

The girl was injured on the chest and covered with blood. She had no shoes on her feet. Still able to think clearly she avoided the many splintered things on the road and trudged towards her home where her family was waiting for her.

Passing through Matoba section, the girl and I came to the area called Kojin-machi Akebono-cho. On both sides of the road there were temples. Everywhere was a sea of fire. No road was open for us anymore except for a narrow path and that was barely passable. The clothes which we earlier had dipped in water had already dried so much that they were almost at the point of burning. There was no time to lose. We dipped our clothes in the water that was stored in an air-raid shelter, and dashed through the fires desperately.

"Awfully hot! Is this the end of my life?...Oh God!...Help me!" I murmured and prayed.

When we managed to come to a safer place, we looked back at the path we had dashed through. It was the most frightful scene I had ever witnessed in my life. Yet even at this safer place, I found many dead bodies lying in the air-raid shelter, under fallen trees, and everywhere.

When we finally arrived at the girl's home at Nakayama section, the darkness of the summer's night was already falling upon us.

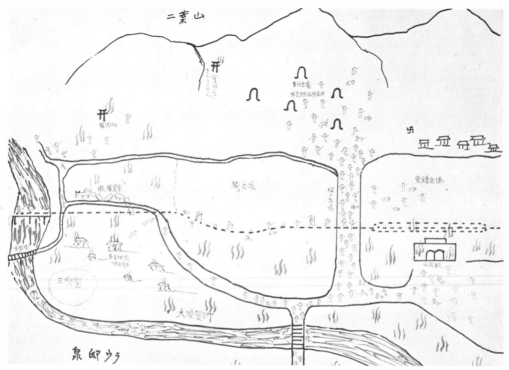

Magoichi Jitsukuni age 69 (93)

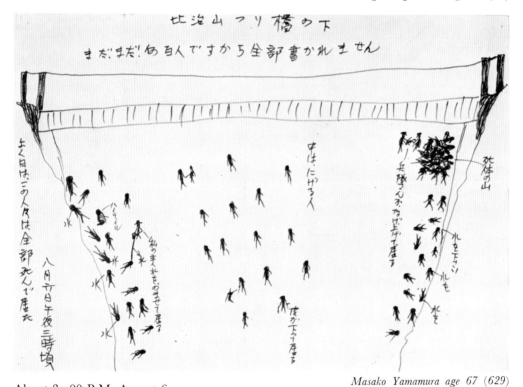

Masako Yamamura age 67 (629)

About 3 : 00 P.M. August 6
Under Hijiyama suspension bridge
In reality several hundred people, not all
drawn, were fleeing.
Next day these people were found dead.

Kishie Masukawa died in 1975 (901)

Members of the neighborhood council from Yamane section of Hiroshima were working on the west approach to the Tsurumi Bridge for the Volunteer Corps on that day. When the A-Bomb exploded, they were blown by the blast into the river and carried by the ebbing tide to the east approach of the Hijiyama Bridge some 1200 feet away. There were cries of "Please help, teacher"; "To the river", and "God help me".

Yoshimi Ikeda age 51 (851)

1. The skin of her hands was burned, swollen, and hanging down.
2. A piece of wood stuck out of her right eye and she seemed to be very much in pain. She walked almost unconsciously.
3. I gave her a cucumber which she held with her left hand.
4. Give me water.
5. Please give me water.
6. Please give me water.
7. Mommy.
8. (Title of picture) On the bank of the Koi River.

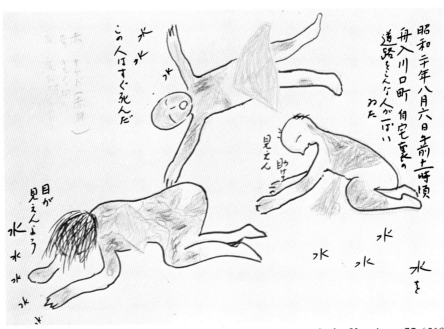

Ayako Uesugi age 77 (516)

At about 11 : 00 A.M. on August 6, 1945 on the road along the back of my house in Funairi-Kawaguchi-cho, there were a lot of people that looked like this.
"Help me ! I can't see anything."
"Water, water ! Give me some water !"
"Water ! I can't see anything."

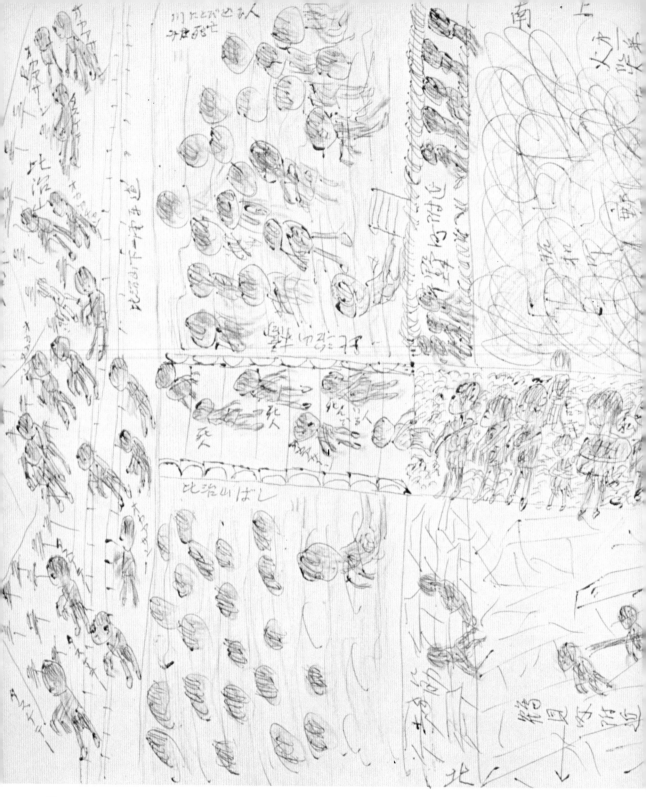

Foot of Mt. Hiji
Streetcar road
Help !   Mommy !

Mt. Hiji Bridge
People who jumped into
the river and died.
corpse

Hirano-machi
neighborhood

Showa-machi
The fire started here.
Post office

Tsurumi-machi
neighborhood
The man under
the roof beam

The A-Bomb exploded when I was near Takara-machi.

A person who was running away from Fujimicho toward Mt. Hiji.

Pieces of window glass all over his face

Big face

Kimiyo Higaki age 76 (270)

Taisho market neighborhood

Takara-machi

Rei Ishii age 48 (35)

Yokogawa Bridge above Tenma River, August
6, 1945, 8 : 30 A.M.
People crying and moaning were running to-
wards the city.   I did not know why.
Steam engines were burning at Yokogawa Sta-
tion.
Tail of cow tied to wire.
Skin of girl's hip was hanging down.
"My baby is dead, isn't she ?"

Sawami Katagiri age 76 (284)

At the Aioi Bridge

On August 9, 1945, I walked around the city looking for my husband. There were many burned persons at each evacuation center. Their injuries were quite extraordinary. I was walking among many dead people. I was too shocked to feel loneliness for my husband. It was like hell. The sight of a living horse burning was very striking. This picture shows only a part of Hiroshima. The whole city was just like this at that time.

Kishiro Nagara age 72 (39)

They headed for Koi Elementary School.
She could not see through the black rain.
"Don't die, my brother !"

(title of picture) The memories of the A-Bomb at that time, Kishiro Nagara, 2–7–4 Koi-kami, Hiroshima city.

About 9:00 A.M., August 6, 1945 in the neighborhood of the Shinjo Bridge about 1 kilometer from Hiroshima City.

Voluntary labor corps suffering from deadly burns were returning home ; others were escaping in a hurry to the outskirts of the city ; many were seeking water on the other side of the river ; some were lying under the bamboo thicket, completely exhausted from walking.

Masao Kobayashi age 77 (549)

A group of junior high school girls seeking shelter were all naked.
Teacher! Teacher! Teacher!
A sense of responsibility.

A junior high school student whose hair had fallen out except where he had worn a cap.

They were tired out when they were caught in the rain.

I am 78 years old. I was living at Midorimachi on the day of the A-Bomb blast. Around 9 : 00 A.M. that morning, when I looked out of my window, I saw several women coming along the street one after another toward the Hiroshima Prefectural Hospital. I realized for the first time, as it is sometimes said, that when people are very much frightened hair really does stand up on end. The women's hair was, in fact, standing straight up and the skin of their arms was peeled off. I supposed they were around 30 years old.

Asa Shigemori age 81 (234)

Kazuo Matsumuro died in 1977 (919)

On the stairs in front of the statue of Fleet Admiral Kato in Hijiyama Park

Although we were lying side by side we did not recognize each other. He heard my voice and said, "Are you Mr. Matsumuro?" It was Mr. Yoshimoto. His face was dark and swollen. He seemed unable to open his eyes or mouth. The left side of his face, neck, and hands, were burned. Soon we were separated.

I was bleeding from my ears, nose, and mouth and was wounded from being crushed. I learned later that the twelfth backbone and the first lumbar vertebra were fractured. I could hardly move.

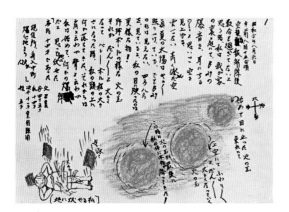

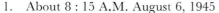

1. About 8 : 15 A.M. August 6, 1945

As I looked up at the sky from the backyard of my house, I heard the faint buzzing of a B–29 but the plane was not visible. A few minutes later, the all clear was sounded. The sun was glaring in the cloudless summer sky. I looked up and suddenly saw a strange thing. There was a fire ball like a baseball growing larger becoming the size of a volleyball. And then something fell on my head. I realized it was something like a bomb showering my body. At that time I was 14 years old.

2. How many seconds or minutes had passed I could not tell but regaining consciousness I found myself lying on the ground covered with pieces of wood. When I stood up in a frantic effort to look around there was darkness. Terribly frightened I thought I was alone in a world of death and groped for any light. My fear was so great I did not think anyone would truly understand. When I came to my senses I found my clothes in shreds and I was without my "geta" (wooden sandals).

3. Suddenly I wondered what had happened to my mother and sister. My mother was then 45 and my sister 5 years old. When the darkness began to fade I found that there was nothing around me. My house, the nextdoor neighbor's house, and the next had all vanished. I was standing amid the ruins of my house. No one was around. It was quiet, very quiet, an eerie moment. I discovered my mother in a water tank. She had fainted. Crying out, "Mamma, Mamma", I shook her to bring her back to her senses. After coming to my mother began to shout madly for my sister, "Eiko, Eiko !"

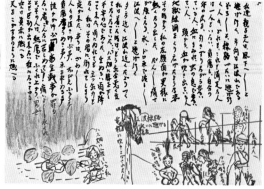

4. I wonder how much time had passed when there were cries of searches. Children were calling their parent's names, and parents were calling the names of their children. We were calling desperately for my sister and listening for her voice and looking to see her. Suddenly Mother cried, "Oh, Eiko!" Four or five meters away my sister's head was sticking out and was calling my mother, "Oka-chan! I'm here!" "Haruko, Eiko is over there!" my mother shouted to me. We ran to save my sister. She was crushed under the collapsed house and only her head could be seen. "How terrible! Be patient! We'll get you out now." Mother and I worked desperately to remove the plaster and pillars and pulled her out with great effort. Her body had turned purple from the bruises and her arm was so badly wounded that we could have placed two fingers in the wound. Strange to say, my mother was thankfully not hurt.

I carried my sister on my back while mother was working very hard to remove more plaster and pillars to help those who were crushed under the broken houses. We saw fires start here and there like a devil's hand.

5. We three ran away, heading for Mt. Eba. A crowd of people were running along the street car track. All were wounded. There was a man with his skin trailing; another man was breathing faintly, all blood-stained; a third man had blood spurting out of his head. It was just like hell!

About that time the left side of my face became extraordinarily hot. The pain grew worse and worse. As I walked toward Mt. Eba I would stop and wash it with muddy water. It was almost evening when we approached Mt. Eba. When we arrived I felt so bad I could not stand, but I felt uneasy sitting in a field of lotus. Then lukewarm rain fell. I did not even have enough energy to stand or find shelter and finally I tumbled over. Night came and I could hear many voices crying and groaning with pain and begging for water. Somone cried, "Damn it! War tortures so many people who are innocent!" Another said, "Ouch! Give me water." This person was so burned that we couldn't tell if it was a man or a woman.

The sky was red with flames. It was burning as if scorching heaven.

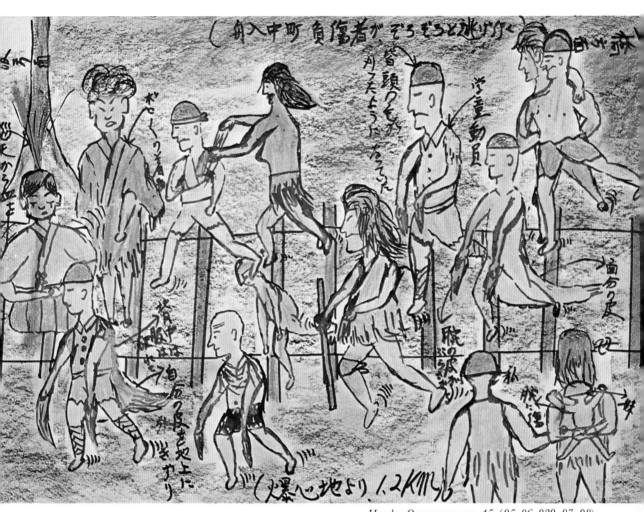

Haruko Ogasawara age 45 (95, 96, 929, 97, 98)

Funairi-nakamachi

1.2 kilometers from the center of the explosion a crowd of the wounded were running away. Some of them had their skin trailing them.

Blood was spurting out of the top of his head. (left)

Clothes torn to shreds. (middle left)

His clothes were torn from his back and his skin was trailing. (bottom left)

Hair seemed to be cut. (right)

Skin was hanging from his arm and trailing his body. (middle right)

Mikio Inoue age 72 (36)

We were on our way home. We were walking along the streetcar line at the foot of Hijiyama. Wherever we went we saw dead horses and bodies lying here and there. The remaining fires were giving off a lot of smoke. Not a soul was in sight. It was when I crossed Miyuki Bridge that I saw Professor Takenaka standing at the foot of the bridge. He was almost naked, wearing nothing but shorts, and he had a rice ball in his right hand. Beyond the streetcar line, the northern area was covered by red fire burning against the sky. Far away from the line, Ote-machi was also a sea of fire.

That day Professor Takenaka had not gone to Hiroshima University and the A-Bomb exploded when he was at home. He tried to rescue his wife who was trapped under a roof-beam but all his efforts were in vain. The fire was threatening him also. His wife pleaded, "Run away, dear !" He was forced to desert his wife and escape from the fire. He was now at the foot of Miyuki Bridge.

But I wonder how he came to hold that rice ball in his hand ? His naked figure, standing there before the flames with that rice ball looked to me as a symbol of the modest hope of human beings.

京橋町 にて

Kazuhiro Ishizu age 68 (371)

Kinzo Nishida age 82 (654)

The day the A-Bomb was dropped

It was about 9 : 30 A.M., August 6, 1945. While taking my severely wounded wife out to the riverbank by the side of the hill of Nakahiro-machi, I was horrified, indeed, at the sight of a stark naked man standing in the rain with his eyeball in his palm. He looked to be in great pain but there was nothing that I could do for him.

I wonder what became of him. Even today, I vividly remember the sight. It was simply miserable.

三滝山

昭和20. 8. 6. 9時30分
新庄町附近をアゴが取れて舌が出
助けを求めて郡部へ北上中
黒い大粒の雨が降っている中を歩い
ている婦人 果してこの人の生命は。

Terumi Nishida age 65 (774)

August 6, 1945, 9 : 30 A.M.
    A woman with her jaw missing and her tongue hanging out of her mouth was wandering around the area of Shinsho-machi in the heavy, black rain. She was heading towards the north crying for help. I wonder if she survived.

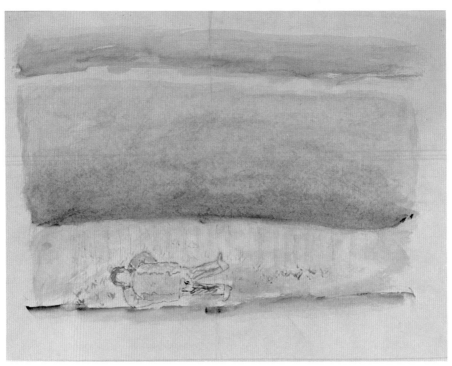

Shigematsu Kajiyama died in 1974 (51)

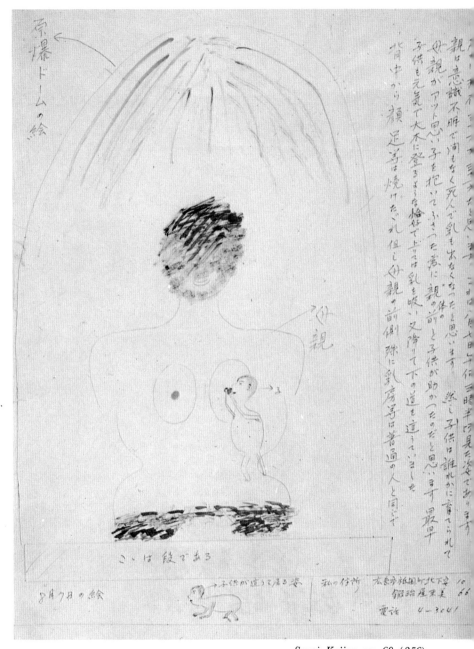

Suemi Kajiya age 69 (256)

The mother's entire back was burned but her front was not injured. Her breasts, especially, appeared normal so that her baby was clinging to them to suckle. The baby was strong and moved from his mother's breasts to the ground and back again. I guessed that she had lain face down with her baby under her body because her front side and her baby remained unburned. She was unconscious. I was afraid she would die soon and the baby's milk would be stopped. If the baby had been saved, and brought up he would be 30 or 31 now. This is what I saw 3 : 30 P.M., August 7.

51

About 8 : 00 A.M., August 7, on the street in front of the former Hiroshima Broadcasting Station

Since I was at school in Ujina I had been exposed to radiation separately from my parents. The next morning at 7 : 30 I started from school toward the ruins of my house in Nobori-cho. I passed by Hijiyama. There were few people to be seen in the scorched field. I saw for the first time a pile of burned bodies in a water tank by the entrance to the broadcasting station. Then I was suddenly frightened by a terrible sight on the street 40 to 50 meters from Shukkeien Garden. There was a charred body of a woman standing frozen in a running posture with one leg lifted and her baby tightly clutched in her arms. Who on earth could she be ? This cruel sight still vividly remains in my mind.

八月七日午前八時頃の旧広島放送局（上流川町）前の路上。

学校へ行ていた為両親と別々に被爆した私は翌七日朝七時宇品から比治を越え観町、私の家の焼跡へもどった。一面の焼野原で人影もまばら。私が始めて真黒に焼けこげに死体を見ひろ旧放送局入口横の水槽の中に折り重そうる教体だった。それから四・五十米縮景園よりの路上に私は異様なものを見てギョッとした。近づいて見ると赤ちゃんを一つかり両手に抱りた女性らうる真黒焦げの片足を上げた走る姿のままこの死体！この人は一件誰だったか。現在もなお鮮明に私の脳裏に残そうる無残で光景である。

広島市段厚栗浦町八一五

山岸康子

Yasuko Yamagata age 49 (495)

白島町 縮景園の裏門に通りかかった
時一人の男の幼児が 門にすがって泣いて
いた。声をかけてさわって見ると 彼は
死んでいた。吾ガ子と思えば胸がつまる。

Name unknown (848)

Walking around the back gate of Shukkeien Garden of Hakushima-cho, I saw an in-
fant boy leaning against the gate and heard
him crying. When I approached and then
touched him, I found that he was dead. To
think that he might have been my son made
my heart ache.

Kiyoko Nishioki age 39 (686)

Around noon of August 6, 1945

This is the scene of the courtyard of the present Hiroshima Prefectural Hospital formerly the Kyosai Hospital. The girl sitting in the center is me. I was gazing at my mother and younger brother who were both totally burned. My brother died around noon before my eyes. A baby in this picture was clinging to his dead mother. He probably died the next day as he was lying rather still beside his mother. The young boy in front of the baby died after saying to me, "I am from Hiroshima First Middle School. Please hand this lunch to my mother." He entrusted me with his Hinomaru Bento, a lunch of rice and plum.

Sumako Yamada age 54 (443)

August 10, 1945
At Honkawa Elementary School
　Two little girls about 3 and 5 years old were cooling their seriously injured mother with paper fans.

Hiroshi Shindo age 65 (193)

Kizo Kawakami age 71 (349)

本堂

八月七日午前十時頃
南観音町眞宗學寮庭
避難して来た人らしくこん
な恰好で死亡しておた。

母親らしく双手で子供を抱いて
ゐる恰好してゐた死んでゐた。
全身褐色に丸々膨れ上り顔
まま空に向け息苦しそうに
して居た。

南側入口

少し若い女性

乳のみ児

Yoshitada Mitsuta age 73 (178)

About 10 : 00 A.M., August 7, at the yard
of the school dormitory of Shinshu Buddhist
sect in Minami Kannon-machi three people
who looked like refugees were found dead as
shown in this picture.

A woman who seemed to be the mother
of a baby was dead. Her arms were curved as
if still holding her baby. Her body was swollen very round. Her face, looking upward,
had the expression of someone who was having
difficulty in breathing.

惨！赤惨！
4名の女子の慌て
・心打たれる物言わぬ
号のしかばね……！
……
膨れ裂引かれた……！
跡が流れて……！
犠牲の血の海……
……
眠と霞う母子の最後
……
水桶の半一杯に
膨れ境けた敵に
砕かれた血に染まれ
青運に凄惨！
……
さまよう河群に、
つどう小女の屍体、
蕾で散った、
女子学生従隊
=）

Unpin Motoyama age 76 (380)

Miserable, so miserable !
countless silent forms of corpses
wringing and shaking our hearts :

A dead horse
abdomen swollen and torn,
entrails bleeding and forming
a pool of blood around :

The last moment of a mother and a child,
too horrible to cast a look ;
Their bloody faces,
swollen and burnt,
crushed in water bucket,
exhibits a horror in blue and black :

Corpses of girls,
collected on the river bank,
where they used to wander ;
these students of the volunteer corps,
now are gone,
without seeing their days.

八月八日　昼前焼跡に帰って来た時の様子

向こう左一軒おいて私の家でした

Shigeko Motooka age 64 (301)

Before noon August 8, 1945, Kannon Town, I returned to the ruins after the fire. My house was the second one on the left.

An old neighbor lady with palsy had been bedridden and burned to death. Only the still smoldering flesh of her abdomen remained.

Another woman who had fled with her baby returned home to search for her older son she had been forced to leave behind. By removing roof tiles, she found the bones of her boy at the bottom of the ruin.

The Kannon Bridge sank in the middle. (upper)
A person dipped his face into a water tank. (upper middle)
At the foot of the bridge, a dead mother is leaning on a pillar. (right side)

Name unknown, housewife, (932)

At Meiji Bridge

A mother, driven half-mad while looking for her child, was calling his name. At last she found him. His head looked like a boiled octopus. His eyes were half-closed, and his mouth was white, pursed, and swollen.

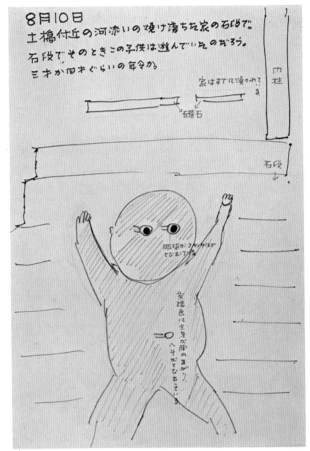

August 10

    At the stone steps of a collapsed house along the riverside near the Dobashi area lay this child. Perhaps he had been playing on the stone steps. He must have been three or four years old.

    Eyeballs popped out about 3 centimeters. His body was swollen and had turned a brown color. His navel protruded.

Jinichi Fujimoto age 47 (23)

August 6, after 5 : 00 P.M.

    In front of the broadcasting station in Nagarekawa I saw a strange thing. There was no doubt that it was a mother and a child burned black.

Tadao Inoue age 67 (641)

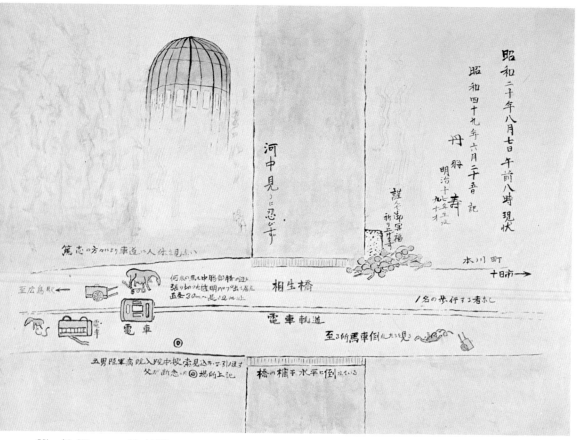

Hisashi Niwa age 93 (197)

August 7, 1945 about 8 : 00 A.M.
Aioi Bridge
It was too horrifying to look into the river.
I prayed for these dead people.
The area was deserted.
This horse's intestines were laying on the ground, clear and puffy, 3 centimeters in diameter by about 2 meters in length.
Freight from horse carts was scattered over the road.
Streetcar tracks
Streetcars turned over.
My fifth son was in the army hospital and at this spot ⊙ I gave up looking for him.
Flattened concrete bridge railing

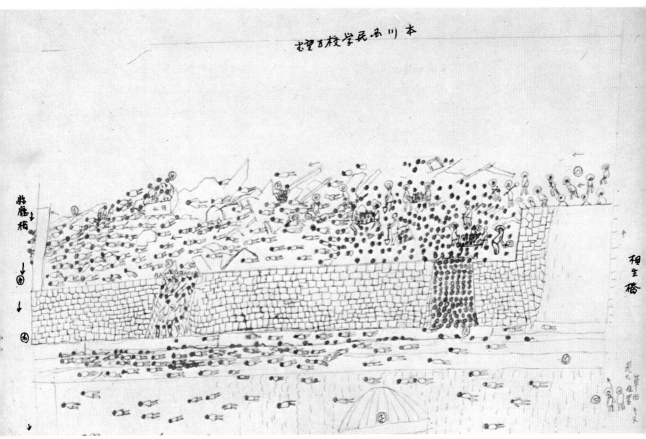

Kinu Kusata age 73 (599)

Honkawa Elementary School

Here, three foreigners were dead.

Aioi Bridge

Location from which Kinu Kusata
viewed this scene.

Kazuhiro Ishizu age 68 (373)

Kaitaichi area
"Oh Praise to Great Buddha"
 A woman cycling into Hiroshima City.
She was going to rescue her child who was in
the Volunteer Corps.

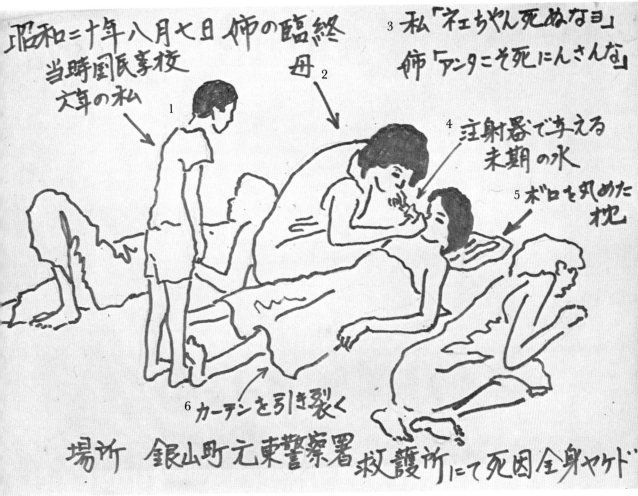

昭和二十年八月七日 姉の臨終
当時国民学校
六年の私　　　1
母　2

3 私「ネェちゃん死ぬなヨ」
姉「アンタこそ死にんさんな」

4 注射器で与える
末期の水

5 ボロを丸めた
枕

6 カーテンを引き裂く

場所　銀山町元東警察署
救護所にて死因全身ヤケド

Name unknown (576)

My sister expires, August 8
1. I, the sixth grader of primary school
2. Mom
3. I : "Never die, never !" Sis. : "You should be the last to die !"
4. The last drip of water given by a injector
5. Pillow made up of rags
6. Torn-off curtain
The place : Motohigashi Police Station in Ginzan-machi
Died of total burn

Masato Une age 80 (685)

A first year junior high school student asked me to give him some water. I heard that if people who had been exposed to the A-Bomb drank water, they would die. So, I would not give him water.

The next day, when I passed by the place, he was lying on the ground dead. I wished then that I had let him drink some water, even if he would have died sooner. I clasped my hands and chanted a prayer to Amitaba. I started to worry even more about my own child, for whom I was looking. He might have died in such a miserable condition or be suffering pain. I left there wiping away the tears which welled up in my eyes.

I heard in the evening that my child had been calling "Daddy", "Mommy" and that he had taken his last breath alone without seeing us. That was the short life of a thirteen-year-old!

It is twenty-nine years since my son died, and his memory, and the miserable image of the junior high school boy asking for water always haunts me.

Oh, the hateful A-Bomb!

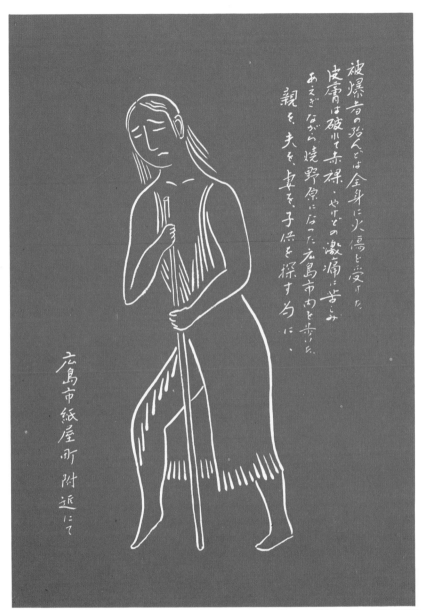

被爆者の殆んどは全身に火傷を受けた。
皮膚は破れて赤裸・やけどの激痛に苦しみ
あえぎながら焼野原になった広島市内を歩いた。
親を、夫を、妻を、子供を探す為に、

広島市紙屋町附近にて

Kazuo Akiyama age 66 (518)

Most of the A-Bomb survivors were burned all over their bodies. They were not only naked, but also their skin came off. Suffering from the severe pain of the burns, they were wandering around looking for their parents, husbands, wives, and children in the city of Hiroshima which had been reduced to ashes.
......Near Kamiyacho in Hiroshima......

S.20.8.7. A.M 8.00頃
竹屋町附近
(爆心地より 0.8Km)

Kazuo Matsumuro died in 1977 (922)

August 7, 1945, 8 : 00 A.M., Takeya section
8 kilometers from the hypocenter. In search
of a place to cremate her dead child.
　　The burned face of the child on her back
was infested with maggots. I guess she was
thinking of putting her child's bones in a
battle helmet she had picked up. I feared she
would have to go far to find burnable material
to cremate her child.

70

死んだ子供を どこで焼こうかしら……

背中にぶらさげた子供の顔の火傷跡には白い「ウジ虫」が動いていた。 拾った鉄カブトは、子供の骨を入れるつもりだろう。

よほど遠くまで行かねば、焼く材料となる物は全くない

S 49.8. 松室一雄（61才）

Sadako Kimura age 77 (176)

71

Yuji Ichida age 64 (398)

Tadao Inoue age 67 (642)

八月七日午後三時頃比治山橋を通ろうと
母親より、婦人が大きなお腹をして死ん
ひゐるそばで三才位の女の子が空詰の
空缶に水を汲んで来て母親の口元れ当て
かぶ子供のいぢらしい姿ん、私は思わず
女の子を抱うよせてお母ちゃんは死んひゐるのよ
と其れ泣きました

瀬川きくの
（67才）

45
3560

Kikuno Segawa age 69 (593)

    I was walking along the Hijiyama Bridge about 3 : 00 P.M. on August 7. A woman, who looked like an expectant mother, was dead. At her side, a girl of about three years of age brought some water in an empty can she had found. She was trying to let her mother drink from it.

    As soon as I saw this miserable scene with the pitiful child, I embraced the girl close to me and cried with her, telling her that her mother was dead.

Iwao Fukui age 61 (702)

When the A-Bomb was dropped I was an army ambulance sergeant of Akatsuki 4039 Corps stationed at Ninoshima Island. I saw this scene when our rescue squad was departing for Hiroshima from Ninoshima Pier. About half an hour after the A-Bomb dropped small ships and barges filled with wounded began arriving at Ninoshima. Some people were towed in the water by rope lashed to their bodies and to the stern of the boats. Of course, they were dead when they were pulled on shore. I did not know whether or not they had already died when they left Hiroshima or whether they had died while being towed by boats too crowded with the injured. But I still remember that miserable sight of the dead bodies with white faces washed in sea water.

Sagami Ogawa age 60 (664)

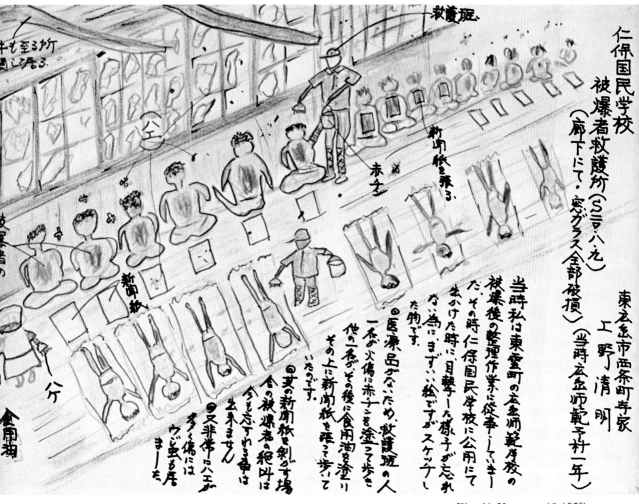

Kiyoaki Ueno age 46 (850)

August 9, 1945, when I was a freshman at the Hiroshima Teacher Training School.

After the A-Bomb dropped I helped in the clean-up and reorganization of the Hiroshima Teacher Training School in Shinonome Town. This is only a sketch of what I saw at the Niho Elementary School when I went there on an errand. I cannot forget the scene I witnessed.

Since there was no medicine, one of the rescue party was coating a survivor's burn with mercurochrome, another coated it with cooking oil, and the third person pasted newspaper over it. I cannot forget the victim's cries at the time the paper was being torn off! As there were a lot of flies, maggots were crawling in the wounds.

The corridor of Niho Elementary School was being used for a survivors' rescue station even though all the windowpanes were broken.

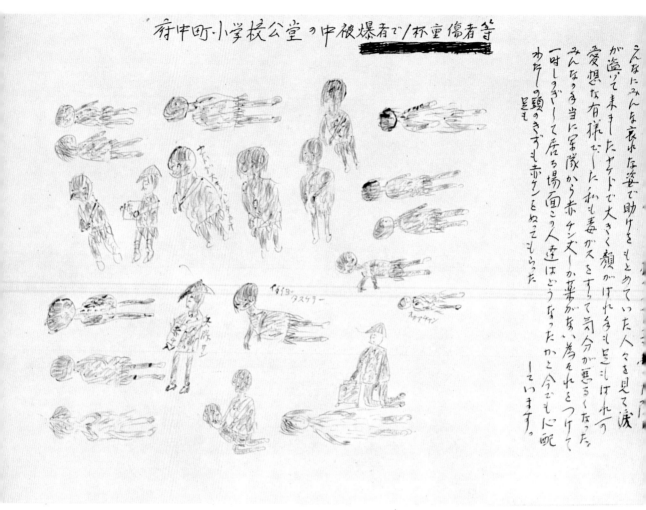

府中町小学校公堂の中被爆者で/杯童傷者等

えんなにみんな哀れな姿で助けをもとめていた人々を見て涙
が盗けて来ましたヤミドで大きく顔がけれ子もとれ/の
愛想な有様でした私も毒がスをすって気分が悪るくなった
みんなう子当に軍隊から赤チン丈一か薬が方へ為それをつけて
一時しのぎして居ち場面こう人達はどうなったかと今でも心配
わたしの頭のきずも赤ケンをぬってもらった
―ています。

Kimiyo Higaki age 76 (271)

While fleeing toward Ogawara I stopped at the auditorium of Fuchu Elementary School. Seeing so many people badly injured and asking for help, I could not help crying myself. It was terrible to see people with their faces, hands, and legs so badly swollen. I also felt sick from inhaling noxious gases. The army had no medicine except mercurochrome and it was, at best, a temporary treatment. Even now I am anxious about what happened to those people. I also had some mercurochrome put on the injury to my face.

Fumie Enseki age 56 (572)

Yoshimi Hara age 58 (22)

散布後、金輪島より大竹海兵団に
被爆者を運ぶ。
引船一隻に団のやうな門橋五隻、
一つ門橋に下士官一名・兵三名・救援
の竹深約三千名・被爆者五十名、
水を与えるが稀一杯なた。止血帯
かはずれて動脈から新しい血が飛
娘さん、口を動かせば教がスイカを割
ったやうなら人、こんな舟五隻に看
護兵一名なのた。
朝五時に出航午后一時に大竹着た
その時敵飛来襲・機用砲撃要
し、何の術も無く毛布をかけるのみ
その門五十名中二名死亡。一名は上
ノ方

After a few days we carried the injured people who had been on Kanawa Island to the Otake Marine Corps Base. Each motorboat pulled five rafts as this picture shows. On each raft were one noncommissioned officer, three soldiers, fifty injured people, and about twenty of their relatives taking care of them. We could do nothing for the injured people but give them water. A girl spurted blood from her artery when her pressure bandage was taken off. There was a man whose face looked like a broken watermelon whenever he moved his mouth. There was just one medical orderly on five of such rafts !

We set sail at five in the morning and were to arrive at Otake at one in the afternoon. Suddenly an enemy plane flew toward us and shot at us with machine guns. We could do nothing but put blankets over the people. During the attack, two of the fifty people were killed. One was a man of fifty from Kaminobori-cho who got up, crawled a few feet while calling for his wife, and then died. I heard later that his wife was taken in another unit and died also. The other of the two was a girl with her family near her.

八月六日.広島市高
須の病院.何百人を
亡う人が医師に手当
を一つとらうために来
てゐた全身焼けた
れた全身体に赤チン
をぬった.

Satoru Yoshimoto age 44 (353)

August 6, 1945 at a hospital in Takasu

Hundreds of people had come to receive some treatment. The doctors were putting mercurochrome on the entirely burned bodies of these people.

My burn immediately after the A-Bomb explosion, August 6, 1945

At that time medicine was scarce. A large number of injured people gathered in a line and were treated with cucumbers, cooking oil, or mercurochrome.

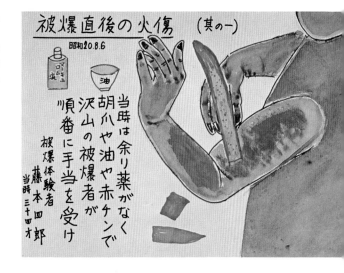

Festering several weeks later

I scraped the festering skin again and again with a knife. Health care : use persimmons and figs ; no smoking ; no alcohol ; plain foods ; take dokudami-grass (a bad-smelling weed) ; avoid oily foods.

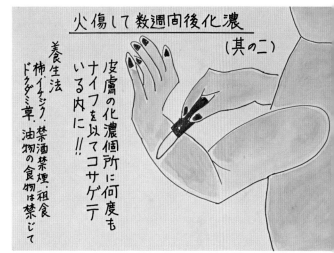

My own treatment miraculously cured my burn.

By scraping with a knife, my skin returned to its normal condition and hair, about six centimeters long, grew out.

I was hit by the A-Bomb on a street in Misasa Town.

Shiro Fujimoto age 66 (498–500)

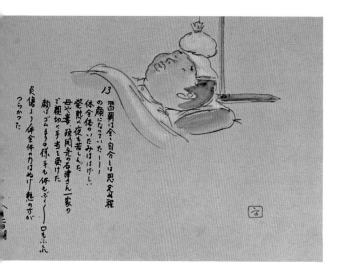

The morning of August 7, 1945

I awoke to find my face terribly changed as if it was not my face. My whole body ached. I suffered from a fever during the night. My mother, wife, and the Ishizu family in whose house we lived during evacuation, kindly took care of me. My face, especially my mouth, felt like a rubber ball. My body did too. The fever, which robbed me of all energy, was more unbearable than the injury.

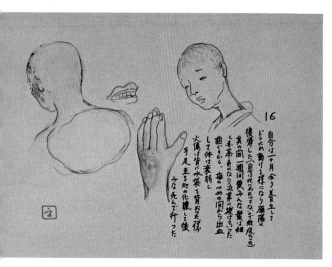

After one month in bed I managed to walk again and so I rejoined my military unit. (As I had not been directly exposed to the bomb-flash, my illness was not too serious.) Within a week all my comrades' hair turned a red-brown color and fell out. They were also bleeding from the gums and under the nails. Gradually they became emaciated and their burns festered all over. It looked like they were carrying bags of water on their backs. They all soon died.

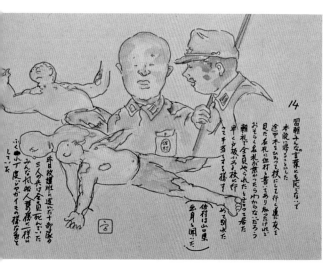

Yoshio Takahara age 66 (144, 145, 147)

I decided to return to Hon-in against the advice of my friends. On the way I met Mr. Samura, a friend of mine. Without his name plate I could not have identified him. He said that all his companions were killed during a morning assembly. I advised him to go to Hesaka Elementary School for medical treatment. Then we parted.

Three soldiers who were brought here by the ambulance squad yesterday had all died. Each of them was swollen like a balloon doll and their skins were the color of potatoes.

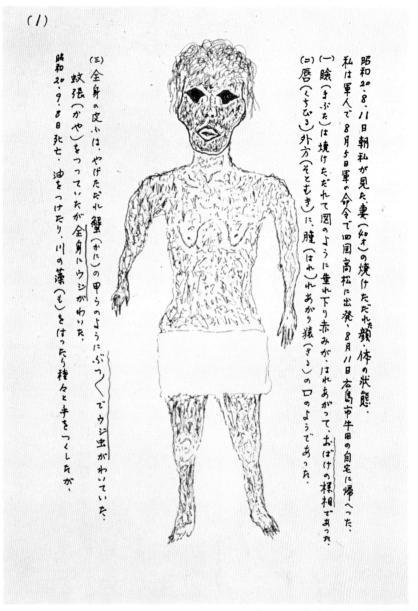

Fusataro Tanimine age 77 (900)

The condition in which I found my 40 year old wife on the morning of August 11, 1945. She was badly burned and had developed running sores.

I was a soldier and had left for Takamatsu in Shikoku by orders of the Army on August 5. So I returned home to Ushita in Hiroshima City.

1. She looked just like a ghost because her eyelids were badly burned and swollen.
2. Her lips, swollen and protruding, made her mouth look like a monkey's.
3. Although she was under mosquito netting, the skin of her whole burned body on which maggots were breeding had the appearance of the crust of a crab.

She died on September 8, 1945, even though I applied oil, seaweed, and tried every other means I could think of to save her life.

Fumiko Yamaoka age 50 (734)

Ken Nakagawa age 64 (540)

This picture is about the rescue operation along the riverbank in Sakaimachi at 8:40 A.M., August 6, 1945. Navy personnel started to rescue people in Honkawa, Enomachi, and Motomachi. There were cries for help from women, children, and old people pinned under houses or crushed between pillars. The fire spread so rapidly that 280,000 people died from burning, asphyxiation, drowning, and being crushed.

The dead were sacrificed for their country. Children, wives, fathers, and friends never came back. I hear phantom voices crying for help. I can not forget.

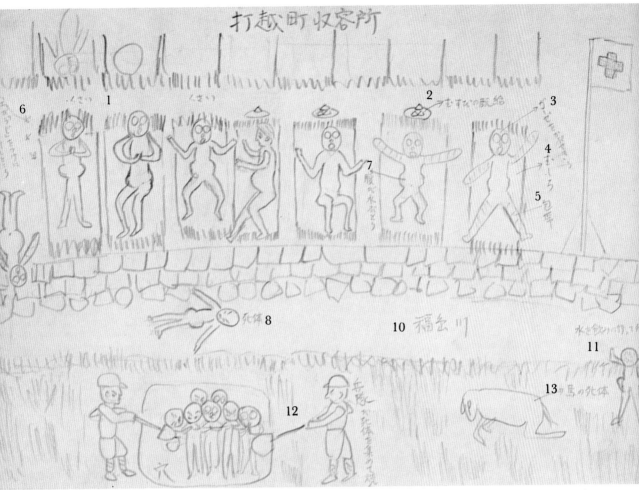

Fusako Suma age 44 (34)

Uchikoshi town's evacuation center
1. Smelled bad
2. Distributed rice balls
3. His face was covered with gauze.
4. Carpet made of straw
5. Bandage
6. Flies caused maggots to form on the wounded people.
7. His stomach was swollen and filled with water.
8. A corpse
9. A corpse
10. Fukushima River
11. He died as he was about to drink water.
12. A hole.......The soldiers gathered and burned the corpse.
13. A dead horse

Yoshiko Tokutomi age 66 (243)

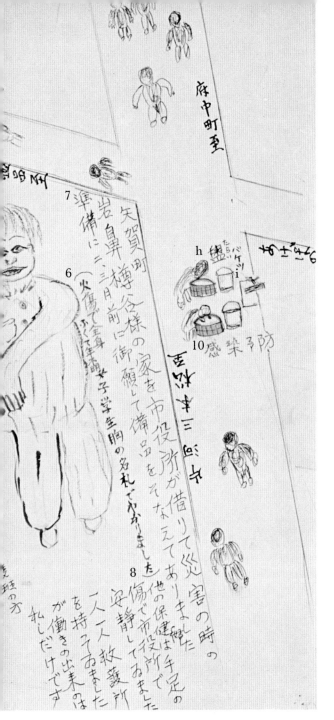

1. As my feet hurt after walking on tiles and broken glass, I picked up gaiters, rolled them into bandages, and wrapped them around my feet.
2. Her face was full of splinters of glass. This nail-puller, which I picked up beneath Tsurumi Bridge when the tide was out, was of much use for people like her.
3. Mr. Harada, who had been the X-ray engineer in the Health Council Center, was severely bruised on his chest when his house collapsed.
4. Such a hair style was in fashion among women during the decisive battles of the last war.
5. A member of the rescue party carrying a stretcher.
6. She was so badly burned that I couldn't see how old she was. The name tag on her chest led me to believe she was a schoolgirl.
7. Two or three months before, the City Office had borrowed the house from the Taruyas in Iwabana, Yaga Town and equipped it with things for a possible war disaster unit.
8. Each health nurse was to have a temporary clinic, but I was the only one who was able to work. The hands and feet of all the others were injured and they lay in the City Office.
9. Hiroshima Rescue Station. (on flag)
10. Prevent Infection.

a. bandages
b. gauze
c. chloroform
d. tincture of iodine
e. disinfectant
f. mercurochrome
g. tincture of oil
h. tub
i. bucket

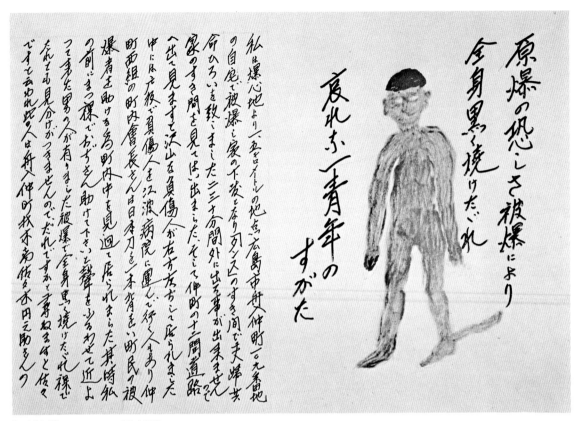

原爆の恐ろしさ被爆により
全身黒く焼けたゞれ
哀れな一青年の
すがた

私は爆心地より一・五キロメートルの地点広島市舟入仲町一〇九番地
の自宅で被爆し家の下敷となり夕ンスのすき間で夫婦共
命からいを致ました二三十分間外に出る事が出来ません
家のすき間を見ては出まった。そして仲町の十二間道路
へ出て見ますと沢山な負傷人が右方左方へと居られました
中には丸裸で員傷人を江波病院に運しに行く人あり仲
町西組の町内會長さんは日本刀を一本背を負い町民ヶ被
爆者圭助ける為町内中を見廻て居られました其時私
の前にまっ裸でおずおずと声をふるわせて近よ
つて来た男久が有りました被爆で全身黒く焼けたゞれ裸で
それでも見分けがつきませんので、だれですか、尋ねますと、佐々
木商店内元助さんク
ですと云われ此人は新入仲の枝木商店元助さんク

Otoichi Yamamoto age 87 (517)

The Terror of the A-Bomb : a miserable young man who was completely burned.

My house was located in Funairi Town, 1.5 kilometers from the hypocenter. There we experienced the A-Bomb and were buried under the house. My wife and I had a narrow escape from death because of space supported by a wardrobe. We could not get out for twenty or thirty minutes but finally found a way through the ruins of the house and crawled out. When we got to the road of Funairi Town, many wounded people were wandering this way and that. Some were carrying the wounded on boards to Eba Hospital. The chairman of the neighborhood organization had a Japanese sword on his back and was patrolling all over the district to help victims of the A-Bomb. Suddenly, one man who was stark naked came up to me and said in a quavering voice, "Please help me !" He was burned and swollen all over from the effects of

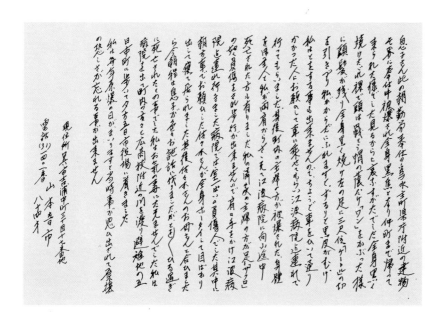

the A-Bomb. Since I did not recognize him as my neighbor, I asked who he was. He answered that he was Mr. Sasaki, the son of Mr. Ennosuke Sasaki, who had a lumber shop in Funairi Town. That morning he had been doing volunteer labor service evacuating the houses near the Prefectural Office in Kako Town. He had been burned black all over and had started back to his home in Funairi. He looked miserable—burned sore, and naked with only pieces of his gaiters trailing behind as he walked. Only the part of his hair covered by his soldier's hat was left, as if he was wearing a bowl. When I touched him, his burned skin slipped off. I did not know what to do, so I asked a passing driver to take him to Eba Hospital.

Soon afterward, I met the wife of my neighbor who had also been injured by the A-Bomb. Although her husband and I tried to help her she died on the way to Eba Hospital.

Another neighbor could not walk because her legs were wounded and looked like pomegranates. We had to take her to the hospital by holding her under her arms. The hospital room was full of wounded people. There I found Mr. Sasaki whom I had met that morning. His entire body, except for his eyes, was covered with bandages. Sometime later I met his mother who was very grateful to me for having helped her son. But she told me he had died just after noon. I was very sorry to hear this.

I left the hospital and went across the river near the Hiroshima Commercial High School with my neighbors. I walked towards Itsukaichi Town where there was a shelter and arrived at the Itsukaichi Town Office in the evening.

Every year, August 6, I remember the time of the A-Bomb explosion. I can never forget the terror and horror of the Atomic Bomb.

Akiko Takakura age 51 (340)

The corpse lying on its back on the road had been killed immediately when the A-Bomb was dropped. Its hand was lifted to the sky and the fingers were burning with blue flames. The fingers were shortened to one-third and distorted. A dark liquid was running to the ground along the hand. This hand must have embraced a child before.

Junjiro Wataoka age 78 (281)

August 7, 1945, 10 : 00 A.M. near Tokaichi-Town streetcar stop

The black hair of a woman streetcar driver remained straight. How strange !

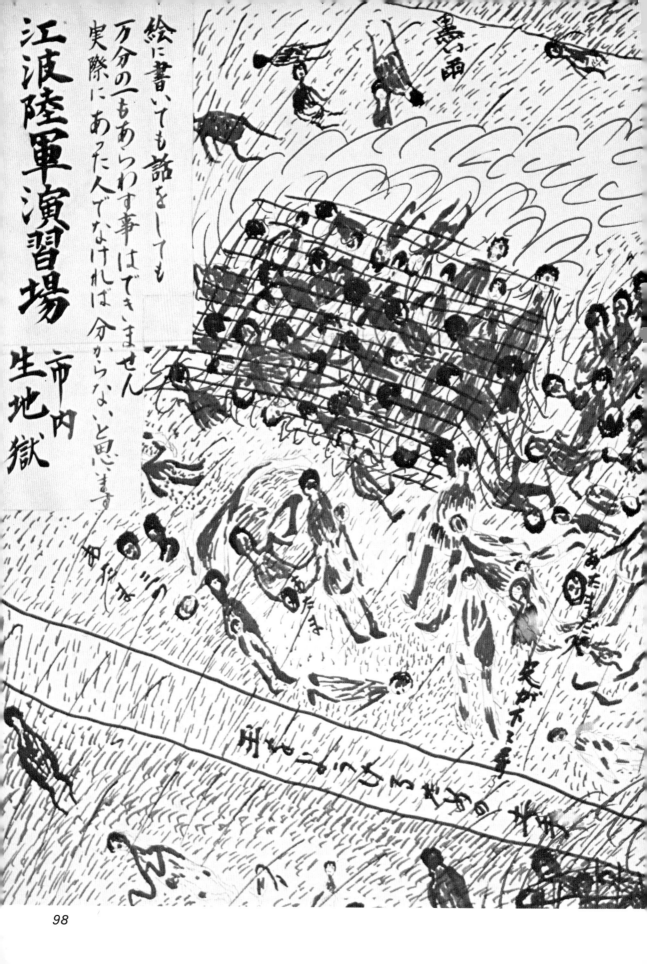

江波陸軍演習場　生地獄

市内

絵に書いても話をしても
万分の一もあらわす事はできません
実際にあった人でなければ分からないと思います

黒い雨

Hamano Matsushita age 73 (268)

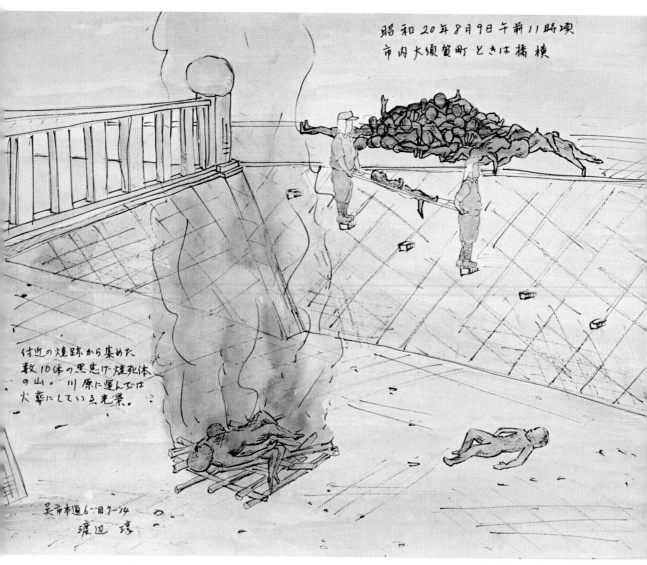

昭和20年8月9日午前11時頃
市内大須賀町ときは橋横

付近の焼跡から集めた
数10体の黒焦げ焼死体
の山。川原に運んでは
火葬にしている光景。

呉市本通6-日7-14
渡辺 瑋

Jun Watanabe age 48 (204)

About 11 A.M. August 9 near the Tokiwa Bridge of Osuka Town

A pile of blackened bodies had been gathered from the nearby ruins. They were being cremated one after another on the riverbed.

◀ **Army Drill Field at Eba**

It was hell on earth all over the city. I don't think I can describe even a ten-thousandth of the reality by drawing a picture or telling a story. I think only those who experienced it can understand.

Black rain was falling.

The labels on the picture indicate mountains of corpses and parts of bodies.

August 6 and 7

At Onaga Town, former east drill field of the army, at the foot of Mt. Futaba. Kokuzen Temple.

Yoshio Hamada age 58 (826) ▶

八月六日

尾長町旧連隊被服兵場ニテ被バクス

広島市　　　　　　　浜田義雄

六十六才

八月六日 午後五時頃、

白島線終点附近

乗客を避難させた後か電鉄の

主任車掌さん制服姿運体状す。

車掌さんは後方で鞄を抱え仰向に倒る。

との側に大八車に凭し倒れいた若い男の遺体一個

右手挙下益に燃えている

左手は通信局

Hidehiko Okazaki age 50 (344)

About 5 P.M. August 6 near the terminal of the Hakushima line

A uniformed streetcar driver lay dead on his stomach. He might have died after leading all the passengers to safety. Beyond the driver, the conductor lay dead on his back still holding his fare bag. A dead young man sitting on a cart beside the tracks was looking up towards the sky. To the right a fire raged along the river bank. To the left was the building of the Communications Bureau.

猿候川におりてたおれる人へ
なかまっ思犯えん帳
8月9日
え 山下正人

Masato Yamashita age 52 (171)

August 9
    With no one to help her, a girl died lean-
ing on the bank of the Enko River.

Masato Yamashita age 52 (170)

August 9

On the west embankment of a military training field was a young boy four or five years old. He was burned black, lying on his back, with his arms pointing toward heaven.

Numbers in the brackets indicate the orders received.

THE PICTURES ABOUT THE ATOMIC BOMB

—AN APPEAL OF THE CITIZENS

This book contains 104 pictures of a total of 975 collected during two months from June to August 1974 in response to an NHK television appeal entitled "Let us Leave for Posterity Pictures about the Atomic-Bomb Drawn by Citizens". None of these pictures was drawn by a professional artist. They were done by old people such as those we pass by in the city of Hiroshima and sit next to on the bus. Most of them had never drawn a picture since their graduation from elementary school. In the pictures the personal experiences of the Atomic Bomb are shown. They are not merely the records and materials of that day thirty years ago. Rather, each picture echoes the heartfelt cry of someone who has been enduring sorrow and suffering for thirty years since the day the Atomic Bomb was dropped.

It Started from a Single Picture

One day in May, 1974 Mr. Iwakichi Kobayashi, an old man of 77 wearing geta, visited the NHK studio in Hiroshima. He had a single picture with him and said that the T. V. drama "Hatoko no Umi," then on the air, reminded him of the Atomic Bomb explosion. He showed us his picture titled "At about 4 P.M., August 6, 1945, near Yorozuyo Bridge". In the simply and vividly drawn picture were countless numbers of people suffering from burns and thirsting for water. There was also a figure of a young lady covered with a burned sheet of tin-roofing lying on the river bank. Mr. Kobayashi explained that he was at the railway station when the Atomic Bomb exploded. He was looking for his only son when he witnessed the scene he had drawn. Usually we think of the Yorozuyo Bridge as an ordinary bridge we cross and we do not pay any attention to it because Hiroshima has many rivers with similar bridges. So we were awed by the extraordinary power of Mr. Kobayashi's picture and by the vividness of his memory even after almost thirty years. How different this was from understanding the Atomic Bomb experience by reading a story. The picture appealed directly to our senses. Mr. Kobayashi said to us, "Even now I can not erase the scene from my memory. Before my death I wanted to draw it and leave it for others." Having heard his words we made up our minds to ask the people who experienced the Atomic Bomb to draw pictures of what they remembered on that day

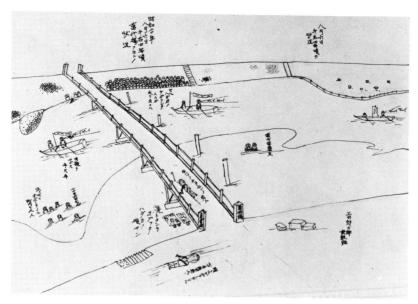

which no other people really know. Just as Mr. Kobayashi was 77 years old we knew that other sufferers of the Atomic Bomb were rapidly aging. Even in Hiroshima the number of people who did not experience the Atomic Bomb had increased to almost half the population. If the Atomic Bomb experience was not recorded soon, it would fade away with this one generation.

NHK broadcasted in June, 1974, a local morning program titled "A Single Picture" which was based on Mr. Kobayashi's drawing. With that program we started an appeal "Let us Leave for Posterity Pictures of the Atomic Bomb Drawn by Citizens". We could not predict whether the sufferers, especially the old people, would draw any pictures as they did not usually draw.

The Movement Spreads

As soon as the program ended, pictures were collected one after another. It was as if a dam had broken. Half the pictures were sent by mail while the other half were brought directly to NHK, some by old people who could hardly walk. Some traveled a long way to the studio and we hardly had time to receive and thank them properly. One said, "I cannot forget this scene." Others showed their pictures explaining them feverishly, sometimes in tears. The pictures were drawn with all kinds of tools such as pencils, crayons, water colors, magic pens, colored pencils, and India ink. The people used almost any kind of paper they could find such as drawing paper, backs of calendars, advertising bills, and paper used for covering sliding doors. Some drew the pictures on the backs of children's scribbled papers, probably those of their grandchildren.

Many trained artists have drawn the miserable scene of that day. But did you know that so many ordinary people could draw pictures like these? Even in Hiroshima it is said that people are apt to forget their experiences of many long years ago. These pictures, however, tell us that survivors cannot forget their experiences.

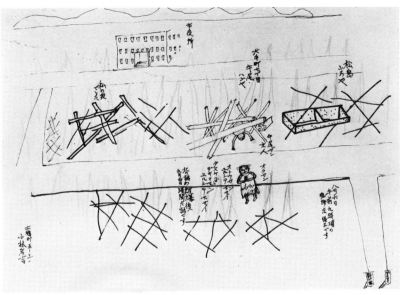

We have mentioned on this television program and also on the news and in announcements that the pictures about the A-Bomb drawn by survivors should be preserved. They were sent not only from Hiroshima Prefecture but also from other prefectures. Riding his motorcycle through a storm wearing a soaked raincoat, Mr. Shiro Fujimoto (p. 85) brought his picture from his home in Fuse town, Yamaguchi Prefecture, 70 kilometers away. When we saw his picture we were astonished to find how graphically it told us of his experience.

Haruko Ogasawara (p. 43) and Tomoko Konishi (p. 12) drew the actions of that day with a series of pictures showing the times of their occurrence. The explanations and the pictures of Hatsuji Takeuchi (p. 28) and Ayako Uesugi (p. 35) make it almost possible to hear the cries of these suffering people.

Almost every picture has an explanation, either on the picture itself, on the backside of it, or on an attached sheet of paper. When the picture does not tell the whole experience, the written explanation helps. Using two colors, one of which is used for drawing the scene before the explosion, the other for immediately after the explosion, the picture on page 24 tells you that the students standing in a line in a morning assembly were blown down by the blast and the heat rays. Keep in mind when you look at this picture that the artist's idea is to make unforgettable his memory of the scene. So, imaginative devices not ordinarily employed by artists have been used to produce these drawings.

Nine hundred pictures were collected before July 1974 and exhibited in Peace Memorial Museum August 1–6, 29 years after the A-Bomb. During that time about 20,000 people saw the pictures. They were asked to write their impressions in notebooks and eighteen were filled. Someone wrote, "We have never seen such an exhibition that shows so many crudely done pictures as this. But these drawings made a stronger impression on us than any others ever did."

The Message the Pictures Wish to Convey

The Assembly Hall used for the exhibition should have been twice the size originally planned for. So many pictures were sent in and even during the exhibition many more pictures arrived. A number of pictures were drawn at the Assembly Hall. The planned space was entirely filled, and later the walls were filled from floor to ceiling.

While we watched people continue to bring in pictures during the filming of the television program about the A-Bomb, we wondered why so many pictures were drawn in spite of their crude techniques. Then we realized that many explanations on the pictures ended with the words "gashoo" or "gashoonembutsu" meaning praying hands or folded hands in prayer for the dead. "I am not good at painting. I am very sorry that I couldn't make a picture scroll which would really tell you of the experience that I had at that time. However, today I drew a picture and wrote an explanation while in front of a Buddhist altar", Mrs. Kinu Kusata explained on her picture.

The pictures convey what the survivors would like, known that in drawing the picture it led them to make amends individually for the people who died that day and to relieve the anguish of their souls. This was related to the positive wish that others should understand the truth of that day. As Mrs. Tsuneyo Masada, age 75, explained of the many blameless people who wanted water, writhed in agony, and died, "I'm an old woman and not good at writing and drawing but in spite of that I was struck with the idea of drawing a picture and writing an explanation so that many people can understand my experience." Many pictures were drawn by people in their sickbeds. Mrs. Katsu Kawano, age 82, drew five pictures with her palsied hands. "I drew a picture with my disabled hands. The scene shows only a part of the misery in my mind from the actual experience." When we went to interview Mrs. Hamano Matsushita about the explanation of her pictures she was seated in her work room and said with great irritation, "This picture could not possibly tell you all my experiences. Even if I drew one hundred pictures, they could not tell you of my experiences !" As they drew their pictures, the sufferers were impatient and dissatisfied because they could not express their real feelings. Drawing reminded them of their painful experiences of 30 years ago. "My hands are trembling and my heart throbs as I think of how I should explain the reality of that situation so that you can really understand," said Mrs. Michiyo Azuma, age 68. While we collected information from the survivors we were deeply impressed by each of their pictures. These pictures cried directly to each viewer of the pain and destruction suffered. They did so not because of their artistry but because of the emotions expressed.

Conclusion

"These pictures are poor in quality if you judge them for artistic quality and techniques. We don't want you to see them as exhibits in a museum. We want to tell you that these things actually happened, that people really died in terrible pain." So wrote 59 year old Mr. Kazuo Kambara.

During the short time in which these pictures were drawn the spread of nuclear weapons has accelerated. Nuclear tests have been made in many countries of the world including India, which recently conducted its first nuclear test. But through the pictures of the A-Bomb sufferers, outsiders can be opened to the long closed world of the first victims of nuclear war and learn that these pictures condemn the folly of nations blindly pursuing a nuclear arms race. These pictures should not be ignored. They will be valuable only when widely shown to people who do not fully understand the Atomic Bomb. We hope that you will grasp the heartfelt cries of every picture for they are truly the starting point of an appeal for peace.

We started to receive pictures again beginning this April, 1975. We received 300 more pictures by the end of May and while we were preparing this book many more pictures were being drawn. Mr. Yoshio Hamada (p. 101) sent us five pictures this year although he is still bedridden. Mrs. Haruko Ogasawara (p. 43) also sent us some pictures. She wrote, "Some of the A-Bomb sufferers are still ill from radiation sickness. I drew pictures again this year because I want to keep handing down that horrible scene of the A-Bombed city which will remain in my memory as long as I live."

For one year, starting with the picture drawn by Mr. Iwakichi Kobayashi we have continued collecting data for our television program. We have been encouraged by the many pictures sent to us and are very sorry that we cannot show you all of them. We too want to pray for the great number of people who died on that day. We express our deep appreciation to those who drew pictures and encouraged us.

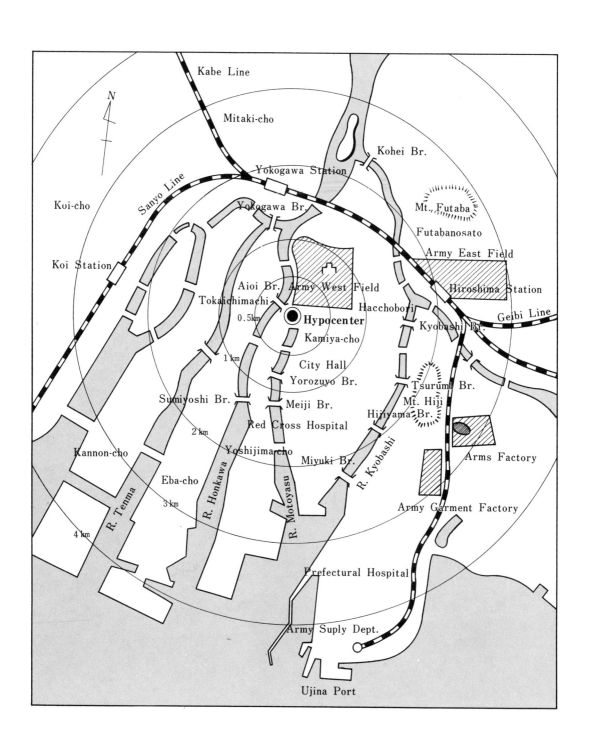

Kabe Line

Mitaki-cho

Kohei Br.

Yokogawa Station

Koi-cho

Sanyo Line

Mt., Futaba

Yokogawa Br.

Futabanosato

Koi Station

Army East Field

Hiroshima Station

Aioi Br. Army West Field

Tokaichimachi

Hacchobori

0.5km

Hypocenter

Kyobashi Br.

Geibi Line

Kamiya-cho

1 km

City Hall

Yorozuyo Br.

Tsurumi Br.

Sumiyoshi Br.

Mt. Hiji

Meiji Br.

Hijiyama Br.

2 km

Red Cross Hospital

R. Kyobashi

Kannon-cho

Yoshijimacho

Miyuki Br.

Arms Factory

R. Tenma

Eba-cho

R. Honkawa

3 km

R. Motoyasu

Army Garment Factory

4 km

Prefectural Hospital

Army Suply Dept.

Ujina Port

name	age	page
Akiyama, Kazuo	66	69
Enseki, Fumie	56	81
Fujimoto, Jinichi	47	63
Fujimoto, Shiro	66	85
Fukui, Iwao	61	76, 77
Hamada, Yoshio	58	101
Hara, Yoshimi	58	82, 83
Harada, Tomoe	52	21, 33
Higaki, Kimiyo	76	36, 37, 80
Hironaka, Torako	63	26, 27
Ichida, Yuji	64	72, 73
Ikeda, Yoshimi	51	34
Inoue, Kiyoshi	51	15, 16
Inoue, Mikio	72	46
Inoue, Tadao	67	63, 74
Ishii, Rei	48	38
Ishizu, Kazuhiro	68	47, 66
Ito, Kanichi	72	28
Jitsukuni, Magoichi	69	30
Kajiya, Suemi	69	51
Kajiyama, Shigematsu died in 1974		50
Katagiri, Sawami	76	39
Kawakami, Kizo	71	57
Kimura, Sadako	77	71
Kiyoyoshi, Goro	80	11
Kobayashi, Iwakichi	80	106, 107
Kobayashi, Masao	77	40
Konishi, Tomoko	58	12, 13
Kusata, Kinu	73	65
Masukawa, Kishie died in 1975		32
Matsumuro, Kazuo died in 1977		42, 70
Matsushita, Hamano	73	98, 99
Michitsuji, Yoshiko	51	29
Mitsuta, Yoshitada	73	58
Motooka, Shigeko	64	60, 61

name	age	page
Motoyama, Unpin	76	59
Nagara, Kishiro	72	40, 41
Nakagawa, Ken	64	90
Nishida, Kinzo	82	48
Nishida, Terumi	65	49
Nishioki, Kiyoko	39	55
Niwa, Hisashi	93	64
Ogasawara, Haruko	45	43, 44, 45
Ogawa, Sagami	60	78
Ojiri, Tsutomu	36	14
Okazaki, Hidehiko	50	19, 102
Sakai, Takehiko	53	20
Segawa, Kikuno	69	75
Shigemori, Asa	81	41
Shindo, Hiroshi	65	56
Suma, Fusako	44	91
Takahara, Yoshio	66	86
Takakura, Akiko	51	96
Takeuchi, Hatsuji	60	28
Tamaru, Yoshiaki	66	18
Tanimine, Fusataro	77	87
Tokutomi, Yoshiko	66	92, 93
Tomita, Atsuko	45	31
Ueno, Kiyoaki	46	79
Uesugi, Ayako	77	35
Une, Masato	80	68
Yamada, Sumako	54	17, 56
Yamagata, Yasuko	49	52, 53
Yamamoto, Otoichi	87	94, 95
Yamamoto, Setsuko	46	22, 23
Yamamura, Masako	67	30
Yamaoka, Fumiko	50	88, 89
Yamashita, Masato	52	103, 104
Yoshimoto, Satoru	44	84
Watanabe, Jun	48	100
Wataoka, Junjiro	78	97
Name withheld by request		24, 25
Name unknown		54, 62, 67

(in alphabetical order)